Wilde Without The Boy

Wilde Without The Boy

A Dramatisation of
Oscar Wilde's *De Profundis*

by

Gareth Armstrong

with the full text of Wilde's
The Ballad of Reading Gaol

The Players' Account
2015

This dramatisation first published in Great Britain in 2015 by
The Players' Account,
an imprint of Cumulus Books,
10 Pattison House, Redcross Way
London SE1 1EY

Designed by Stephen Davies
Printed and bound in Great Britain by
TJ International Ltd, Padstow, Cornwall

A CIP catalogue for this book is available from the British Library

ISBN 978-0-9536647-3-3

CONTENTS

Wilde Without The Boy

INTRODUCTION

Gerard Logan is an actor who likes a challenge. Some years ago he asked me if I thought Shakespeare's epic poem *The Rape of Lucrece* would make a good one-man show. I said no. Gerard is also very persistent. He told me he had learnt it anyway, all 1800 lines of it, and maybe I would listen to him recite it.

The truth was that I had never been able read *Lucrece* all the way through, so this way I could at least tick it off my list of neglected texts. Gerard recited it in my front room. As well as being courageous and persistent he is also a very fine actor. He managed to communicate the poem's narrative, its themes, its moral purpose and most significantly its theatrical potential

It should come as no surprise that anything penned by Shakespeare would take on an extra dimension in the mouth of an actor, but hearing the poem's protagonists brought to life convinced me that I had been wrong to dismiss its potential as a solo theatre piece.

The success of that show has vindicated Gerard's vision and confounded my scepticism.

Gerard next came up with another classic text I had never been quite able to get through. Returning to my front room he read aloud *De Profundis*, the letter Oscar Wilde wrote to his lover Lord Alfred Douglas (Bosie) whilst serving a prison sentence for committing homosexual acts. It has some of the most beautifully written and poignant prose I have ever heard, but it was twice as long as *Lucrece*, had no narrative line, no dramatic shape and only one voice: that of the bruised and often bitter author. Making a play out of a poem seemed like easy work compared with making a play out of a letter.

The first surprise on starting work on a script was that, although Wide had written his letter in 1897, the original manuscript remained unavailable until 1960. Previous versions had been edited for a variety of personal and legal reasons, and even the one published by Wilde's own son, Vyvyan Holland, in 1949 contained hundreds of errors. It was Robert Ross, the friend to whom Wilde handed his text after his release from Reading gaol, who insisted that the original manuscript remain unavailable for fifty years. His motive was to ensure that Bosie, its intended recipient, would never see it in its entirety.

We got hold of several versions of the text and I took myself off to the British Library to look at the original manuscript. Without sufficient notice and an especially compelling reason it is not possible to handle the manuscript itself, but they have a facsimile which is accessible by the ancient technology of microfiche. There are twenty folio-sized pages in Wilde's highly legible hand.

The official prison policy was that an inmate was only allowed one sheet of paper to write on, and that would be removed at the end of the day. When Wilde was writing *De Profundis* the Governor of Reading Gaol was a man called Major Nelson. He was a good deal more sympathetic to his charge than his predecessor had been, and as well as lending him books from his own library he allowed him access to other works. The pages are covered with many crossings out, amendments and additions, but some pages are in fair copy, and most do not end with a full stop. It seems very likely that the one-page-a-day rule was relaxed in Wilde's case. He was also permitted to take the work home with him at the end of his sentence.

Gerard was tasked with coming up with a version of manageable length, and we both agreed that it should last an hour. We didn't always agree on what should go and what should stay however, and over the weeks we often changed our minds and found ourselves fighting from the opposite corner. The most gorgeous prose on the page does not always translate into good monologue, and the pith of a passage can easily be lost among elegant sub-clauses. We soon realised that the final arbiter of what would work theatrically was reading the text aloud to each other, and admitting when the lines no longer held our attention as listeners.

As well as the passages that had to be sacrificed for reasons of length or clarity there was the question of structure. The first challenge was to invent a context for the performance. The knowledge that Wilde was given the manuscript on his release gave us the excuse for him to review his handiwork whilst waiting for freedom. A sort of anteroom or holding cell suggested itself as a location – neither incarcerated nor wholly at liberty. We discovered that the night before his release the prison authorities ordered that he be moved from Reading Gaol in the hours of darkness to Pentonville. This was to confuse the press and those wanting to sensationalise his emergence from prison. The period as he awaited the transportation from one gaol to another was a sort of limbo where Wilde could reflect on the disastrous relationship that had made him a convict in the first place.

Of course the letter assumes knowledge of the background and circumstances of Wilde's fall from grace, but the play would need to fill in the blanks for people less familiar with the story. References to his court appearances gave us the opportunity to include dramatised scenes from the trials using recorded voices for the judge, the prosecutor and a witness. Letters from Bosie's enraged father, the Marquess of Queensberry, and the infamous poem that mentions 'the love that dares not speak its name' also added texture and background material to the script.

In such a heartfelt epistle it is hardly surprising that sentiments are repeated and that particular subjects recur from time to time. We certainly exercised dramatic licence in editing these and occasionally combined passages from different sections of the text to reinforce them or to give them a stronger theatrical impetus. I would like to think the consummate playwright in Wilde might have approved of these changes, and although working with a dead writer has huge advantages when you are taking liberties with a text there were days when we would have loved to consult him.

'A blacker, fiercer, falser, craftier, more grovelling or more abominable piece of writing never fell from a mortal pen.' That verdict on *De Profundis* from the journalist TWH Crosland represents the views of many of Wilde's detractors, though it can hardly be regarded as dispassionate literary criticism as Crosland was a friend of Lord Alfred Douglas. Gerard and I decided that we would rather side with Richard Ellmann's assessment of the work. He wrote a magisterial biography of Wilde in which he described it as 'a love letter…one of the greatest, and the longest ever written.'

Without disguising the recrimination, the bitterness and the occasional intellectual snobbery that the letter contains we wanted to honour it as a genuine outpouring from a poetic soul to someone whose beauty and potential had captivated him to the point of obsession. We also wanted to try and capture the essence of the man who was such an artistic and social phenomenon of his time, and to reflect the mythic status he now holds amongst dizzyingly disparate sections of society. This goes beyond Wilde's words and demands the recreation of the man's spirit.

Of all the sources we tapped in search of this spirit the one that spoke most eloquently to Gerard and me were these brief sentences from H. Montgomery Hyde. 'Oscar was no tragedian. He was the superb comedian of his century, one to whom misfortune, disgrace, imprisonment were external and traumatic. His gaiety of soul was invulnerable.'

Gareth Armstrong, 2015

The first performance of *Wilde Without the Boy* was given at the Buxton Festival on Sunday July 20th 2014. *

Oscar Wilde	Gerard Logan
Director	Gareth Armstrong
Composer	Simon Slater

* Gerard Logan won Best Actor (Buxton Festival Fringe) for this performance.

Wilde Without The Boy

May 25th 1895. The Royal Courts of Justice at the Old Bailey, London.

A projection of The Royal Coat of Arms appears.

A chair, upstage left, representing the dock is brightly lit.
Justice Wills pronounces sentence on Oscar Wilde (Voice Over).

Justice Wills   *Oscar Fingal O'Flahertie Wills Wilde, the crime of which
you have been convicted is so bad that one has to put stern
restraint upon oneself to prevent oneself from describing, in
language which I would rather not use, the sentiments which
must rise in the breast of every man of honour who has
heard the details of these two horrible trials. That the jury
has arrived at a correct verdict in this case I cannot persuade
myself to entertain a shadow of a doubt; and I hope, at all
events, that those who sometimes imagine that a judge is
half-hearted in the cause of decency and morality because he
takes care no prejudice shall enter into the case, may see that
it is consistent at least with the utmost sense of indignation at
the horrible charges brought home you.*

*It is no use for me to address you. People who can do these
things must be dead to all sense of shame, and one cannot
hope to produce any effect upon them. It is the worst case I
have ever tried. That you, Wilde, have been the centre of a
circle of extensive corruption of the most hideous kind among
young men, it is impossible to doubt. I shall, under the
circumstances, be expected to pass the severest sentence that
the law allows. In my judgement it is totally inadequate for
a case such as this. The sentence of the Court is that you be
imprisoned and kept to hard labour for two years*

13

Wilde
Off Stage

And I? May I say nothing, my Lord?

> The Coat of Arms fades, and an anteroom in Reading Gaol is revealed with the chair representing the dock upstage left. To the right of downstage centre is a plain wooden table and chair. The furniture is institutional.
>
> On the table is an oil lamp and a brown paper package secured with black ribbon. Tucked under the ribbon is an envelope.
>
> Wilde enters, not knowing why he has been told to wait here. He is smartly dressed in grey with a bottle green cravat and carries no hat or cane. He takes in his surroundings and notices the package on the table. He removes the envelope from under the ribbon.

WILDE
(Reading)

'Prisoner C33'

> He opens the envelope and reads the letter enclosed.

'17th of May 1897
'Tonight, during the hours of darkness, you are to be transferred from Her Majesty's Prison here in Reading to Her Majesty's Prison, Pentonville, from whence you will be released at the completion of your sentence. This procedure is intended to confound and confuse the gentlemen of the press and others who would seek to sensationalise your return to freedom.

'Please find enclosed a Postal Order in the amount of 10 shillings, given in goodwill from her Majesty's Government.

'I am also empowered to return to you this manuscript, written with my consent, during your incarceration.

Major James Osman Nelson (Governor)'

A good and humane man.

Wilde places the letter on the table, where it will serve as all the correspondence in the play. He pulls at the ribbon to reveal its contents, extracts the first page and reads.

'Dear Bosie,
'After long and fruitless waiting I have determined to write to you myself, as I would not like to think that I had passed through two long years of imprisonment without ever having received a single line from you, or any news or message even, except such as gave me pain.

He is distressed and returns the page to its packaging. After some indecision he returns to the manuscript and continues reading.

'I have no doubt that in this letter in which I have to write of your life and of mine, there will be much that will wound your vanity to the quick. If it prove so, read the letter over and over again. It is the only thing that can save you, though each word may become to you as the fire or knife of the surgeon that makes the delicate flesh burn or bleed. Remember also that whatever is misery to you to read, is still greater misery to me to set down.

'Where you will receive this letter, if indeed it ever reaches you, I don't know. Rome, Naples, Paris, Venice...'

The manuscript is now a stage property, as Wilde lifts his eyes from the page and addresses Bosie.

...you are surrounded, if not with all the useless luxury you had with me, at any rate with everything that is pleasurable to eye, ear, and taste. Life is quite lovely to you. And yet, if you are wise, and wish to find life much lovelier still and in a different manner, you will let the reading of this letter prove to you as important a crisis and turning-point of your life as the writing of it is to me. The supreme vice is shallowness. Whatever is realised is right.

I was a man who stood in symbolic relations to the art and culture of my age. The gods had given me almost everything. I had genius, a distinguished name, high social position, brilliancy, intellectual daring. Whatever I touched I made beautiful in a new mode of beauty. I awoke the imagination of my century so that it created myth and legend around me: I summed up all systems in a phrase, and all existence in an epigram.

Along with these things, I had things that were different. I let myself be lured into long spells of senseless and sensual ease. I surrounded myself with the smaller natures and the meaner minds. I became the spendthrift of my own genius. Tired of being on the heights I deliberately went to the depths in the search for new sensations. People thought it dreadful of me to have entertained at dinner the evil things of life, and to have found pleasure in their company. It was like feasting with panthers! The danger was half the excitement. They were intensely interesting. They were to me the brightest of gilded snakes! What I do feel ashamed of is the horrible Philistine atmosphere into which you brought me.

My business as an artist was with Ariel. You set me to wrestle with Caliban. There is where I found myself after two years' friendship with you, right in the centre of Philistia, away from everything that was beautiful, or brilliant, or wonderful, or daring. I allowed you to dominate me, and your father to frighten me. There is only one thing for me now, absolute Humility.

Everything that has happened to me I have to transform into a spiritual experience. There is not a single degradation of the body which I must not try and make into a spiritualising of the soul. For just as the body absorbs things of all kinds, things common and unclean no less than those that the priest or a vision has cleansed, and converts them into the play of beautiful muscles and the moulding of fair flesh, so the Soul has its nutritive functions also, and can transform into noble moods of thought, and passions of high import, what in itself is base, cruel, and degrading: nay more, may find in these its most august modes of assertion, and can often reveal itself most perfectly through what was intended to desecrate or destroy.

And the first thing that I have got to do is to free myself from any possible bitterness of feeling against you. Religion does not help me. When I think about Religion at all, I feel as if I would like to found an order for those who cannot believe: the Confraternity of the Fatherless one might call it, where on an altar, on which no taper burned, a priest, in whose heart peace had no dwelling, might celebrate with unblessed bread and a chalice empty of wine.

I shall really have no difficulty in forgiving you. But to make it a pleasure for me you must feel that you want it. When you really want it you will find it waiting for you.

I will begin by telling you that I blame myself terribly. As I sit here in this dark cell in convict clothes, a disgraced and ruined man, it is myself I blame. I blame myself for allowing an unintellectual friendship, a friendship whose primary aim was not the creation and contemplation of beautiful things, to entirely dominate my life.

From the very first there was too wide a gap between us. High thoughts and high emotions are by their very existence isolated. You couldn't know, you couldn't understand, you couldn't appreciate. Your interests were merely in your meals and moods. It was only in the mire that we met: and fascinating, terribly fascinating though the one topic round which your talk invariably centred was, I was often bored to death by it.

In one of the violent letters you wrote to me, you said that you were under 'no intellectual obligation of any kind to me'. That was the one really true thing you had written to me in the whole course of our friendship. I saw that a less cultivated nature would really have suited you much better. Your lack of any power of sustained intellectual concentration, that you had not been able to acquire the Oxford temper, never been one who could play gracefully with ideas but had arrived at violence of opinion merely – that all these things, combined with the fact that your desires and interests were in Life not in Art, were as destructive to your own progress in culture as they were to my work as an artist.

You admired my work when it was finished: you enjoyed the brilliant successes of my first nights, and the brilliant banquets that followed them: but you could not understand the conditions requisite for the production of artistic work. I am not speaking in phrases of rhetorical exaggeration but in terms of actual truth to actual fact, when I remind you that during the whole time we were together I never wrote one single line. Whether at Torquay, Goring, London, Florence or elsewhere, my life, as long as you were by my side, was entirely sterile and uncreative. And with but few intervals you were, I regret to say, by my side always.

When you were away I was all right. While you were with me you were the absolute ruin of my Art. Deliberately and by me uninvited you thrust yourself into my sphere, usurped there a place for which you had neither right nor qualifications, and succeeded in absorbing my entire life – could do no better with that life than break it in pieces. Strange as it may sound to you, it was but natural that you should do so. If one gives to a child a toy too wonderful for its little mind, it breaks the toy. So it was with you. Having got hold of my life, you did not know what to do with it. You couldn't have known. It was too wonderful a thing to be in your grasp. You should have let it slip from your hands and gone back to your own companions at their play. But unfortunately you were wilful, and so you broke it.

I blame myself again for having allowed you to bring me to utter and discreditable financial ruin. I remember one morning in the early October of 1892 sitting in the yellowing woods at Bracknell with your mother. The conversation turned on you and your mother began to speak to me about your character. She told me of your two chief faults, your vanity, and your being as she termed it 'all wrong about money'. I have a distinct recollection of how I laughed. I had no idea that the first would bring me to prison and the second to bankruptcy. But you outstripped all taste and temperance. You demanded without grace and received without thanks. When I tell you that between the autumn of 1892 and the date of my imprisonment I spent with you and on you more than £5000 in actual money, irrespective of the bills I incurred, you will have some idea of the sort of life on which you insisted.

You forgot the grace of sweet companionship, the charm of pleasant conversation, and all those gentle humanities that make life lovely. Letting you squander my fortune to your own hurt as well as to mine, gives to me and in my eyes a note of common profligacy to my Bankruptcy, that makes me doubly ashamed of it. I was made for other things.

But most of all I blame myself for the entire ethical degradation I allowed you to bring on me. The basis of character is will-power, and my will-power became absolutely subject to yours. It was the case of that tyranny of the weak over the strong which somewhere in one of my plays I describe as being 'the only tyranny that lasts'. Those incessant scenes that seemed to be almost physically necessary to you, and in which your mind and body grew distorted and you became a thing as terrible to look at as to listen to: that dreadful mania you inherit from your father for writing revolting and loathsome letters: your entire lack of any control over your emotions - these, I say, were the origin and causes of my fatal yielding to you in your daily increasing demands. I had allowed you to sap my strength of character. Ethically you had been even more destructive to me than you had been artistically.

And the curious thing to me is that you should have tried to imitate your father in his chief characteristics. I cannot understand why he was to you an exemplar, where he should have been a warning. I remember quite well your saying to me with your most conceited air that you could beat your father 'at his own trade'. Quite true. But what a trade!

At the one supremely and tragically critical moment of all my life, just before my lamentable step of beginning my absurd legal action against your father, on the one side there was your father attacking me with hideous cards left at my club, on the other side there was you attacking me with no less loathsome letters. I saw no possible escape. Spurred-on by your taunts, to take an action against your father and have him arrested, the last straw to which I clutch in my wretched efforts to escape is the terrible expense. You said that your mother's rich relations themselves would look on it as a real delight to be allowed to pay all costs and expenses that might be incurred in any such effort. I had no excuse left for not going. I was forced into it.

You were wrong even in fancying that it would have been an absolute delight and joy to your mother if you had managed through me to get your father put into prison. I feel sure you were wrong. And if you want to know what a woman really feels when her husband, and the father of her children, is in prison dress, in a prison cell, write to my wife and ask her. She will tell you. I confess that it pains me when I hear of your mother's remarks about me, and I am sure that on reflection you will agree with me that if she has no word of regret or sorrow for the ruin your race has brought on mine it would be better if she remained silent. Of course there is no reason she should see any portion of this letter that refers to any mental development I have been going through, or to any point of departure I hope to attain to. It would not be interesting to her. But the parts concerned purely with your life I should show her if I were you.

The arrest warrant for your father once granted, your will of course directed everything. At a time when I should have been in London taking wise counsel, you insisted on my taking you to Monte Carlo, of all revolting places on God's earth, that all day, and all night as well, you might gamble as long as the Casino remained open. You refused to discuss even for five minutes the position to which you and your father had brought me. My business was merely to pay your hotel expenses and your losses.

On our return to London those of my friends who really desired my welfare implored me to retire abroad, and not to face an impossible trial. You forced me to stay to brazen it out, if possible, in the box by absurd and silly perjuries. At the end, I was of course arrested.

> **Wilde is standing behind the 'dock' chair. The Royal Coat of Arms is projected and Wilde is highlighted as he listens to the voices at his trial (voice over) of his Prosecutor, CF Gill and a witness, Charles Parker.**

Gill   *You are Charles Parker?*

Parker   *I am. I am 21 years of age. I have been engaged as a valet. At the beginning of 1893 I was out of employment. I remember one day at that time being with my brother at the St James's Restaurant, in the bar. While there Taylor came up and spoke to us. He was an entire stranger. He passed the compliments of the day, and asked us to have a drink. We got into conversation with him. He spoke about men.*

Gill   *Where did you first meet Wilde?*

Parker   *Taylor said he could introduce us to a man who was good for plenty of money and that. He took us to a restaurant in Rupert Street. I think it was the Solferino. We were shown upstairs in to a private room in which there was a dinner table laid for four. After a while, Wilde came in and I was formally introduced. I had never seen him before but I had heard of him. We dined about 8 o'clock.*

Gill   *Was the dinner a good dinner?*

Parker	*Yes. The table was lighted with red shaded candles. We had plenty of champagne with our dinner and brandy and coffee afterwards. Wilde paid for the dinner.*
Gill	*Of what nature was the conversation?*
Parker	*General at first. Nothing was then said about the purposes for which we had come together.*
Gill	*And then?*
Parker	*Wilde said to me, 'This is the boy for me. Will you go to the Savoy Hotel with me?' I consented and Wilde drove me in a cab to the hotel. At the Savoy we went first to a sitting room on the second floor. Wilde then asked me to go in to his bedroom with him.*
Gill	*Let us know what occurred there?*

The Coat of arms cross fades back to the anteroom.

Wilde	Do you think I am here on account of my relations with the witnesses on my trial? My relations, real or supposed, with people of that kind were matters of no interest to either the Government or Society. I am here for having tried to put your father into prison. My attempt failed of course. Your father completely turned the tables on me, and had me in prison, has me there still. That is why there is contempt felt for me. That is why people despise me. That is why I have to serve out every day, every hour, ever minute of my dreadful imprisonment.

Some paper, the *Pall Mall Gazette* I think, describing the dress-rehearsal of one of my plays, spoke of you as following me about like my shadow: the memory of our friendship is the shadow that walks with me here: that seems never to leave me: that wakes me up at night to tell me the same story over and over till its wearisome iteration makes all sleep abandon me till dawn: at dawn it begins again: it follows me into the prison-yard and makes me talk to myself as I tramp round: each detail that accompanied each dreadful moment I am forced to recall: there is nothing that happened in those ill-starred years that I cannot recreate in that chamber of the brain which is set apart for grief or for despair: every strained note of your voice, every twitch and gesture of your nervous hands, every bitter word, every poisonous phrase comes back to me: I remember the street or river down which we passed, the wall or woodland that surrounded us, at what figure on the dial stood the hands of the clock, which way went the wings of the wind, the shape and colour of the moon.

Secretly you must think of yourself with a good deal of shame. A brazen face is a capital thing to show the world, but now and then when you are alone, and have no audience, you have, I suppose, to take the mask off for mere breathing purposes. Else, indeed, you would be stifled.

I should have got rid of you. But my fault was, not that I did not part from you, but that I parted from you far too often. As far as I can make out I ended my friendship with you every three months, and each time that I did so you managed by means of telegrams, letters, the interposition of your friends to induce me to allow you back. After a series of scenes culminating in one more than usually revolting, when you came one Monday evening to my rooms accompanied by two of your friends, I found myself actually flying abroad next morning to escape from you, leaving a false address with my servant for fear you might follow me by the next train. You actually telegraphed to my wife begging her to use her influence with me to get me to write to you. Our friendship had always been a source of distress to her: not merely because she had never liked you personally, but because she saw how your continual companionship altered me, and not for the better: still, just as she had always been most gracious and hospitable to you, so she could not bear the idea of my being in any way unkind. At her request I did communicate with you. Pity, my old affection for you, regard for your mother - all these, if excuses be necessary, made me consent to renew our friendship. Two days after, your father saw you having luncheon with me at the Café Royal, joined my table, drank of my wine, and that afternoon, through a letter addressed to you, began his first attack on me.

Wilde uses the letter from Governor Nelson to represent the Marquess of Queensberry's letter

'I am not going to try and analyse this intimacy, and I make no charge; but to my mind to pose as a thing is as bad [as] to be it.....With my own eyes I saw you both in the most loathsome and disgusting relationship as expressed by your manner and expression. Never have I seen such a sight as in your horrible features. No wonder people are talking as they are.'

And he naturally went further still. He secures by fraud a seat for the first night of one of my plays and contrives a plot to interrupt the performance, to make a foul speech about me to the audience, to throw offensive or indecent missiles at me when I am called before the curtain at the close. By the merest chance, in the brief and accidental sincerity of a more than usually intoxicated mood, he boasts of his intention before others. Information is given to the police, and he is kept out of the theatre.

It may be strange, but I had once again, I will not say the chance, but the duty of separating from you forced on me. I need hardly remind you that I refer to your conduct to me at Brighton in October '94. I was trying to finish my last play at Worthing by myself. The two visits you had paid to me had ended. You suddenly appeared a third time bringing with you a companion whom you actually proposed should stay in my house. I (you must admit now quite properly) absolutely declined. I entertained you, of course; I had no option in the matter: but elsewhere, and not in my own home. The next day, a Monday, your companion returned to the duties of his profession, and you stayed with me. Bored with Worthing, and still more, I have no doubt, with my fruitless efforts to concentrate my attention on my play, the only thing that really interested me at the moment, you insist on being taken to the Grand Hotel at Brighton. The night we arrive you fall ill. I need not remind you how I waited on you, and tended you, not merely with every luxury of fruit, flowers, presents, books, and the like that money can procure, but with that affection, tenderness and love that, whatever you may think, is not to be procured for money. After four or five days you recover, and I take lodgings in order to try and finish my play. You, of course, accompany me.

The morning after the day on which we were installed I feel extremely ill. You have to go to London on business, but promise to return in the afternoon. In London you meet a friend, and do not come back to Brighton till late the next day, by which time I am in a terrible fever, and the doctor finds I have caught the influenza from you. The next two days you leave me entirely alone without care, without attendance, without anything. I could not even get the milk the doctor had ordered for me: and when I begged you to procure me a book at the bookseller, you never even take the trouble to go there. All the while you are of course living at my expense and indeed only appearing in my room for money.

On Saturday night, you having left me completely unattended and alone since the morning, I asked you to come back after dinner, and sit with me for a little. With irritable voice and ungracious manner you promise to do so. I wait till eleven o'clock and you never appear. At three in the morning, unable to sleep, and tortured with thirst, I made my way, in the dark and cold, down to the sitting-room in the hopes of finding some water there. I found you. You fell on me with every hideous word an intemperate mood, an undisciplined and untutored nature could suggest. By the terrible alchemy of egotism you converted your remorse into rage. You accused me of trying to deprive you of your pleasures. In the morning you repeat the same scene with renewed emphasis and more violent assertion. You moved suddenly towards me.

Only once before in my life had I experienced such a feeling of horror at any human being. It was when in my library at Tite Street, waving his small hands in the air in epileptic fury, your father, with his bully between us, had stood uttering every foul word his foul mind could think of, and screaming the loathsome threats he afterwards with such cunning carried out. In the latter case he, of course, was the one who had to leave the room first. I drove him out. In your case I went. It was not the first time I had been obliged to save you from yourself.

I determined never under any circumstances to allow you to enter my house, to sit at my board, to talk to me, walk with me, or anywhere and at any time to be my companion at all. Then as I was sitting at breakfast, I happened to open the newspaper and saw in it a telegram stating that your elder brother had been found dead in a ditch with his gun lying discharged beside him. From the horror of the circumstances of the tragedy, the pathos of the sudden death of one so loved by all who knew him came infinite pity for you and your family. What you had been to me in my sickness, I could not be to you in your bereavement. I opened to you my house, my home, my heart. I made your sorrow mine also, that you might have help in bearing it. Never, even by one word, did I allude to your conduct towards me, to the revolting scenes.

But for my pity and affection for you and yours, I would not now be weeping in this terrible place.

Wilde, seated at the table, rocks back and forth and conjures up the lines from *The Ballad of Reading Gaol*.

…the brave man with a sword…

Yet each man kills the thing he loves
  By each let this be heard.
Some do it with a bitter look,
  Some with a flattering word.
The coward does it with a kiss
  The brave man with a sword…

The anteroom becomes the prison yard where Wilde and fellow prisoners exercise and he intones verses from the Ballad.

With slouch and swing around the ring
  We trod the Fool's Parade!
We did not care: we knew we were
  The Devil's Own Brigade:
And shaven head and feet of lead
  Make a merry masquerade.

We tore the tarry rope to shreds
  With blunt and bleeding nails;
We rubbed the doors, and scrubbed the floors,
  And cleaned the shining rails:
And, rank by rank, we soaped the plank,
  And clattered with the pails.

We sewed the sacks, we broke the stones,
  We turned the dusty drill:
We banged the tins, and bawled the hymns,
  And sweated on the mill:
But in the heart of every man
  Terror was lying still

Wilde sits with his head in his hands in the 'dock' chair. He slowly reasserts himself and continues.

Our friendship really begins with your begging me in a most pathetic and charming letter to assist you in a position appalling to anyone, doubly so to a young man at Oxford. You were being blackmailed over an indiscreet letter. On my instruction and at my expense, my friend and solicitor, George Lewis, accustomed to dealing with such embarrassments, paid the blackmailer a hundred pounds in return for the incriminating document.

Later you send me a very nice poem, of the undergraduate school of verse, for my approval: I reply by a letter of fantastic literary conceits. The letter is like a passage from one of Shakespeare's sonnets, transposed to a minor key.

Governor Nelson's letter again represents Wilde's early letter to Bosie.

'My Own Boy,
'Your sonnet is quite lovely, and it is a marvel that those red-roseleaf lips of yours should be made no less for the madness of music and song than for the madness of kissing. Your slim gilt soul walks between passion and poetry. I know Hyacinthus, whom Apollo loved so madly, was you in Greek days....

'Always, with undying love,

'Yours, Oscar'

Look at the history of that letter! It passes from you into the hands of a loathsome companion. Copies of it are sent about London to my friends, and to the manager of the theatre where my work is being performed: every construction but the right one is put on it. This forms the basis of your father's worst attack: I produce the original letter myself in Court to show what it really is: it is denounced by your father's Counsel as a revolting and insidious attempt to corrupt Innocence. I go to prison for it at last. That is the result of writing you a charming letter.

One day you come to me and ask me, as a personal favour to you, to write something for an Oxford undergraduate magazine, about to be started by some friend of yours, whom I had never heard of in all my life, and knew nothing at all about. To please you – what did I not do always to please you? – I sent him a page of paradoxes destined

30

originally for the *Saturday Review*. A few months later I find myself standing in the dock of the Old Bailey on account of the character of the magazine. It forms part of the Crown charge against me. I am called upon to defend your friend's prose and your own verse.

The former I cannot palliate; the latter I, loyal to the bitter extreme, to your youthful literature as to your youthful life, do very strongly defend, and will not hear of your being a writer of indecencies. But I go to prison, all the same, for your friend's undergraduate magazine, and 'the Love that dares not tell its name'.

The courtroom returns. Wilde is behind the 'dock' chair and begins to read the poem to the court.

> 'Sweet youth,
> Tell me why, sad and sighing, thou dost rove
> These pleasant realms? I pray thee speak me sooth
> What is thy name?' He said, 'My name is Love.'
> Then straight the first did turn himself to me
> And cried,...'

Gill (voice over) interrupts Wilde's reading and continues the poem:

Gill
(Voice over)

> '... *He lieth, for his name is Shame,*
> *But I am Love, and I was wont to be*
> *Alone in this fair garden, till he came*
> *Unasked by night; I am true Love, I fill*
> *The hearts of boy and girl with mutual flame.'*
> *Then sighing, said the other, 'Have thy will,*
> *I am the Love that dare not speak its name.'*

What, Mr Wilde, is the 'Love that dare not speak its name'?

Wilde   The 'Love that dare not speak its name' in this century is such a great affection of an elder for a younger man as there was between David and Jonathan, such as Plato made the very basis of his philosophy, and such as you find in the sonnets of Michelangelo and Shakespeare. It is that deep, spiritual affection that is as pure as it is perfect. It dictates and pervades great works of art like those of Shakespeare and Michelangelo, and those two letters of mine, such as they are. It is in this century misunderstood, so much misunderstood that it may be described as the 'Love that dare not speak its name', and on account of it I am placed where I am now. It is beautiful, it is fine, it is the noblest form of affection. There is nothing unnatural about it. It is intellectual, and it repeatedly exists between an elder and a younger man, when the elder man has intellect, and the younger man has all the joy, hope and glamour of life before him. That it should be so the world does not understand. The world mocks at it and sometimes puts one in the pillory for it.

> The courtroom becomes the anteroom once more and Wilde resumes his address to Bosie.

In you Hate was always stronger than Love. Your hatred of your father was of such stature that it entirely outstripped, o'erthrew, and overshadowed your love of me. Hate, you have yet to learn, is, intellectually considered, the Eternal Negation. Hate blinds people. Love can read the writing on the remotest star. Hate gnawed at your nature, as the lichen bites at the root of some sallow plant, till you grew to see nothing but the most meagre interests and the most petty aims. For two days you sat on a high seat with the Sheriffs, and feasted your eyes with the spectacle of your father standing in the dock of the Central Criminal Court. And on the third day I took his place. What had occurred? In your hideous game of hate together, you had both thrown dice for my soul, and you happened to have lost. That was all.

When an execution was put into my house, and my books and furniture were seized and advertised to be sold, and bankruptcy was impending, I naturally wrote to tell you about it. I did not mention that it was to pay for some gifts of mine to you that the bailiffs had entered the home where you had so often dined. I thought, rightly or wrongly, that such news might pain you a little. You wrote back from Boulogne in a strain of almost lyrical exultation. You said that you knew your father was 'hard up for money', and had been obliged to raise £1500 for the expenses of the trial, and that my going bankrupt was really a 'splendid score' off him as he would not then be able to get any of his costs out of me! That all my charming things were to be sold: my Library with its wonderful array of college and school prizes, its *éditions de luxe*, and the like; was absolutely nothing to you. You said it was a great bore: that was all. What you really saw in it was the possibility that your father might ultimately lose a few hundred pounds, and that paltry consideration filled you with ecstatic joy. Do you realise now what Hate blinding a person is?
You may be interested to know that your father openly said in the Orleans Club that if it had cost him £20,000 he would have considered the money thoroughly well spent, he had 'extracted such enjoyment, and delight, and triumph out of it all'. The fact that he was able not merely to put me into prison for two years, but to take me out for an afternoon and make me a public bankrupt was an extra-

refinement of pleasure that he had not expected. It was the crowning-point of my humiliation, and of his complete and perfect victory.

After my terrible sentence, when the prison-dress was on me, and the prison-house closed, I sat amidst the ruins of my wonderful life, crushed by anguish, bewildered with terror, dazed through pain. But I would not hate you. Every day I said to myself, 'I must keep Love in my heart today, else how shall I live through the day?' There were times, even in those dark days, the darkest of all my life, when I actually longed to console you. So sure was I that at last you had realised what you had done.

It did not occur to me then that you could have the supreme vice, shallowness.

Sorrow after sorrow has come beating at the prison doors in search of me. They have opened the gates wide and let them in. Hardly, if at all, have my friends been suffered to see me. Other miserable men, when they are thrown into prison, can hide in the darkness of their cells, and of their very disgrace make a mode of sanctuary. The world, having had its will, goes its way, and they are left to suffer undisturbed. With me it has been different. On November 13th 1895 I was brought down here to Reading from London. I had been taken out of the Hospital Ward without a moment's notice being given to me. From two o'clock till half-past two on that day I had to stand on the centre platform of Clapham Junction in convict dress and handcuffed, for the world to look at. Of all possible objects I was the most grotesque. When people saw me they laughed. That was of course before they knew who I was. As soon as they had been informed, they laughed still more. For half an hour I stood there in the grey November rain surrounded by a jeering mob. For a year after that was done to me I wept every day at the same hour and for the same space of time. That is not such a tragic thing as possibly it sounds to you. To those who are in prison, tears are a part of every day's experience. It is always twilight in one's cell, as it is always midnight in one's heart. A day in prison on which one does not weep is a day on which one's heart is hard, not a day on which one's heart is happy. Well, now I am really beginning to feel more regret for the people who laughed than for myself. To mock at a soul in pain is a dreadful thing. Unbeautiful are their lives who do it.

Three more months go over, and my mother dies. Her death was so terrible to me that I, once a lord of language, have no words in which to express my anguish and my shame. Never, even in the most perfect days of my development as an artist, could I have had words fit to bear so august a burden, or to move with sufficient stateliness of music through the purple pageant of my incommunicable woe. The messenger of Death has brought me his tidings and gone his way, and in entire solitude, and isolated from all that could give me comfort, or suggest relief, I have had to bear the intolerable burden of misery and remorse that the memory of my mother placed upon me, and places on me still. Even people who had not known me personally, hearing what a new sorrow had come into my broken life, wrote to ask that some expression of their condolence should be conveyed to me.

You alone sent me no message, and wrote me no letter. Why did you not write to me? Was it cowardice? Was it callousness? What was it? Your silence has been horrible.

It is a silence without excuse; a silence without palliation. If you had any imagination in you, you would know that there is not a single person who has been kind to me in my prison-life, down to the warder who may give me a good-morning or a good-night that is not one of his prescribed duties, down to the poor thief who, recognising me as we tramped round the yard at Wandsworth, whispered to me in the hoarse prison-voice men get from long and compulsory silence: 'I am sorry for you: it is harder for the likes of you than it is for the likes of us' - not one of them all, I say, the very mire from whose shoes you should not be proud to be allowed to kneel down and clean.

The poor speak of one who is in prison as of one who is 'in trouble' simply. The phrase has the perfect wisdom of Love in it. The very books in my cell are paid for by Robbie out of his pocket-money. From the same source are to come clothes for me, when I am released. I am not ashamed of taking a thing that is given by love and affection. I am proud of it.

But I had still one beautiful thing left, my own eldest son. Suddenly he was taken away from me by the law. That the law should decide that I am one unfit to be with my own children is something quite horrible to me. It was a blow so appalling that I did not know what to do, so I flung myself on my knees, and bowed my head, and wept and said 'The body of a child is as the body of the Lord: I am not worthy of either.' That moment seemed to save me. I saw then that the only thing for me was to accept everything. Since then – curious as it will no doubt sound to you – I have been happier. It was of course my soul in its ultimate essence that I had reached. In many ways I had been its enemy, but I found it waiting for me as a friend.

Behind Sorrow there is a soul. There is about Sorrow an intense, an extraordinary reality. For the secret of life is suffering. It is what is hidden behind everything. When we begin to live, what is sweet is so sweet to us, and what is bitter so bitter, that we inevitably direct all our desires towards pleasure. There was no pleasure I did not experience. I threw the pearl of my soul into a cup of wine. I lived on honeycomb. But the other half of the garden had its secrets for me also.

I have to speak to you with regard to the conditions, circumstances, and the place of our meeting when my term of imprisonment is over. I understand that you have sealed up in two packages my letters and my presents to you - such at least as remain of either - and are anxious to hand them personally to me. It is, of course, necessary that they should be given up. They belong to a side of life that is long over, to a friendship that somehow you were unable to appreciate at its proper value.

I am to be released, if all goes well with me, towards the end of May, and hope to go at once to some little seaside village abroad with Robbie and More Adey. I hope to be at least a month with my friends, and to gain, in their healthful and affectionate company, peace, and balance, and a less troubled heart, and a sweeter mood. I tremble with pleasure when I think that on the very day of my leaving prison both the laburnum and the lilac will be blooming in the gardens, and that I shall see the wind stir into restless beauty the swaying gold of the one, and make the other toss the pale purple of its plumes so that all the air shall be Arabia for me. At the end of a month, when the June roses are in all their wanton opulence, I will, if I feel able, arrange through Robbie to meet you in some quiet foreign town like Bruges, whose grey houses and green canals and cool, still ways had a charm for me, years ago.

I hope that our meeting will be what a meeting between you and me should be, after everything that has occurred. In old days there was always a wide chasm between us, the chasm of achieved Art and acquired culture: there is a still wider chasm between us now, the chasm of Sorrow: but to Humility there is nothing that is impossible, and to Love all things are easy.

Of course I know that from one point of view things will be made more difficult for me than for others. Society, as we have constituted it, will have no place for me, has none to offer; but Nature, whose sweet rains fall on unjust and just alike, will have clefts in the rocks where I may hide, and secret valleys in whose silence I may weep undisturbed, send the wind over my footprints so that none may track me to my hurt.

Still, in the very fact that people will recognise me wherever I go, I can discern something good for me. It will force on me the necessity of again asserting myself as an artist, and as soon as I possibly can. If I can produce one more beautiful work of art I shall be able to rob malice of its venom, and cowardice of its sneer, and to pluck out the tongue of scorn by the roots.

But I am assured on legal authority that I cannot even publish a book without the permission of the Receiver to whom all the accounts must be submitted. I cannot enter into a contract with the manager of a theatre, or produce a play without the receipts passing to your father and my few other creditors. Even when I am stripped of all I

have, and am ever to have, and am granted a discharge
as a hopeless Insolvent, I have still got to pay my debts.
The dainty cuff-links – four heart-shaped moonstones of
silver mist, girdled by alternate ruby and diamond for their
setting – that I designed, and had made at Henry Lewis's
as a special little present to you, to celebrate the success
of my second comedy - these even - though I believe you
sold them for a song a few months afterwards - have to be
paid for. I cannot leave the jeweller out of pocket for the
presents I gave you, no matter what you did with them. The
Savoy dinners -the clear turtle soup, the luscious ortolans
wrapped in their crinkled Sicilian vine-leaves, the heavy
amber coloured, indeed almost amber-scented champagne
– Dagonet 1880, I think, was your favourite wine? – all
have still to be paid for. The suppers at Willis's, the special
cuvée of Perrier-Jouet reserved always for us, the wonderful
patés procured directly from Strasbourg, the marvellous
fine champagne served always at the bottom of great
bell-shaped glasses that its bouquet might be the better
savoured by the true epicures of what was really exquisite
in life.

Some six weeks ago I was allowed by the Doctor to have
white bread to eat instead of the coarse black or brown
bread of ordinary prison fare. It is a great delicacy. To you
it will sound strange that dry bread could possibly be a
delicacy to anyone. I assure you that to me it is so much
so that at the close of each meal I carefully eat whatever
crumbs may be left on my tin plate, or have fallen on
the rough towel that one uses as a cloth so as not to soil
one's table: and do so not from hunger – I get now quite
sufficient food – but simply in order that nothing should be
wasted of what is given to me.

The only people I would care to be with now are artists and people who have suffered: those who know what Beauty is, and those who know what Sorrow is: nobody else interests me. If after I go out a friend of mine gave a feast, and did not invite me to it, I shouldn't mind a bit. I can be perfectly happy by myself. With freedom, books, flowers, and the moon, who could not be happy? But if, after I go out, a friend of mine had a sorrow, and refused to allow me to share it, I should feel it most bitterly. If he thought me unworthy, unfit to weep with him, I should feel it as the most poignant humiliation, as the most terrible mode in which disgrace could be inflicted on me. But that could not be. I have a right to share in Sorrow, and he who can look at the loveliness of the world, and share its sorrow, and realise something of the wonder of both, is in immediate contact with divine things, and has got as near to God's secret as anyone can get.

And the end of it all is that I have got to forgive you. I must do so. I don't write this letter to put bitterness into your heart, but to pluck it out of mine. If I have brought this pitiless indictment against you, think what an indictment I bring without pity against myself. Terrible as what you did to me was, what I did to myself was far more terrible still.

The sound of the door to the anteroom opening

For yourself, I have but this last thing to say. You came to me to learn the Pleasure of Life and the Pleasure of Art. Perhaps I am chosen to teach you something much more wonderful, the meaning of Sorrow, and its beauty. Your affectionate friend ...

An offstage voice interrupts...

Warder
(Voice over)

Prisoner C33.

Wilde moves towards the exit and announces:

Wilde

Oscar Wilde.

He leaves.

The lights fade to blackout.

The Ballad of Reading Gaol

by Oscar Wilde

INTRODUCTION

The performing time of *Wilde Without the Boy* is a little
over one hour. This suits many national and international
theatre festivals, including the Edinburgh Fringe, where
there are so many options for audiences to choose from and
they want to maximise their theatregoing experience. But
touring venues usually request a longer programme. This
is to give their local audiences better value for their ticket
price, and also provides an interval where theatres and arts
centres can boost their takings with revenue from the bar.

So it was partly for pragmatic reasons that Gerard and
I sought a way to extend our Oscar Wilde evening. *The
Ballad of Reading Gaol* was an obvious choice, as it also
relates to the time of his imprisonment when Wilde wrote
De Profundis.

On the 7th of July 1896 a trooper in the Royal Horse Guards,
Charles Thomas Wooldridge, who had been found guilty
of cutting the throat of his wife Laura Ellen, was hanged
for her murder. The execution took place in the grounds
of Reading Gaol where Wilde was serving his two year
sentence for homosexual offences. The *Ballad* is dedicated
to Wooldridge's memory.

The poem is an unflinching indictment of the Victorian
penal system, particularly the death penalty, and the ballad

form is the ideal medium for recounting and meditating on the brutal realities of such a regime. But its strict metre and regular rhythms also recall the repetitive harshness of prison life as experienced by Wilde and all other inmates. Most crucially, like all traditional ballads it is written to be performed rather than read.

After Gerard had committed the poem to memory, as usual in record time, we sought a context in which to perform it. We discovered that Wilde had written the poem in exile in France after his release from gaol, either in Berneval-le-Grand or in Dieppe. By this time he was a broken man and also very short of cash. There are poignant stories of him trying to borrow money from old acquaintances he meets in the streets to pay his bills or even buy a drink. In our version we find him sitting outside a café in the sunshine and conjuring up the dark days of his imprisonment and the searing memory of Wooldridge's hanging.

The theatre composer Simon Slater and I have worked on over a dozen projects together over the years, and he understands the vital contribution that incidental music can make to a production. Being an actor too, he knows that incidental music is exactly that, incidental, and its primary purpose is to serve the play. Even so, there have been shows of mine when Simon's music has been the most notable element in the production.

Staging the *Ballad* seemed the ideal opportunity to bring Simon's work more to the fore, and he agreed to compose a score for the whole performance. He, Gerard and I worked over a period of months to find the right scope and tone for this underscoring. As well as a prodigious memory Gerard has a fine ear, and we felt we could risk recording the score on a single track lasting some thirty-five minutes. It is a real tightrope for Gerard and leaves not even a beat for a lapse of memory or even a lengthy breath. But these strict poetic and musical metres reinforce the ballad form and, we hope, bring a new dimension to the performance.

Oscar Wilde would never have heard the Ballad recited or performed in his native land. It was published in England in 1898, and brought in a meagre income during the remaining two years of his life. Most poignantly, Leonard Smithers the publisher did not name Wilde as the author, because of his notoriety; but the front cover attributed the work to '*C33. Cell block C, landing 3, cell 3*' - Wilde's identity during his incarceration in Reading Gaol.

Gareth Armstrong

The first performance of *The Ballad of Reading Gaol*, by Oscar Wilde, with an original score by Simon Slater, was given at the Bedford Park Festival on June 25th 2015.

Oscar Wilde :   Gerard Logan

Director: Gareth Armstrong

Composer: Simon Slater

The Ballad of Reading Gaol

by Oscar Wilde

I

He did not wear his scarlet coat,
  For blood and wine are red,
And blood and wine were on his hands
  When they found him with the dead,
The poor dead woman whom he loved,
  And murdered in her bed.

He walked amongst the Trial Men
  In a suit of shabby grey;
A cricket cap was on his head,
  And his step seemed light and gay;
But I never saw a man who looked
  So wistfully at the day.

I never saw a man who looked
  With such a wistful eye
Upon that little tent of blue
  Which prisoners call the sky,
And at every drifting cloud that went
  With sails of silver by.

I walked, with other souls in pain,
  Within another ring,
And was wondering if the man had done
  A great or little thing,
When a voice behind me whispered low,
  'That fellow's got to swing.'

Dear Christ! the very prison walls
  Suddenly seemed to reel,
And the sky above my head became
  Like a casque of scorching steel;
And, though I was a soul in pain,
  My pain I could not feel.

I only knew what hunted thought
  Quickened his step, and why
He looked upon the garish day
  With such a wistful eye;
The man had killed the thing he loved
  And so he had to die.

Yet each man kills the thing he loves
  By each let this be heard,
Some do it with a bitter look,
  Some with a flattering word,
The coward does it with a kiss,
  The brave man with a sword!

Some kill their love when they are young,
  And some when they are old;
Some strangle with the hands of Lust,
  Some with the hands of Gold:
The kindest use a knife, because
  The dead so soon grow cold.

Some love too little, some too long,
  Some sell, and others buy;
Some do the deed with many tears,
  And some without a sigh:
For each man kills the thing he loves,
  Yet each man does not die.

He does not die a death of shame
  On a day of dark disgrace,
Nor have a noose about his neck,
  Nor a cloth upon his face,
Nor drop feet foremost through the floor
  Into an empty place

He does not sit with silent men
  Who watch him night and day;
Who watch him when he tries to weep,
  And when he tries to pray;
Who watch him lest himself should rob
  The prison of its prey.

He does not wake at dawn to see
  Dread figures throng his room,
The shivering Chaplain robed in white,
  The Sheriff stern with gloom,
And the Governor all in shiny black,
  With the yellow face of Doom.

He does not rise in piteous haste
  To put on convict-clothes,
While some coarse-mouthed Doctor gloats, and notes
  Each new and nerve-twitched pose,
Fingering a watch whose little ticks
  Are like horrible hammer-blows.

He does not know that sickening thirst
 That sands one's throat, before
The hangman with his gardener's gloves
 Slips through the padded door,
And binds one with three leathern thongs,
 That the throat may thirst no more.

He does not bend his head to hear
 The Burial Office read,
Nor, while the terror of his soul
 Tells him he is not dead,
Cross his own coffin, as he moves
 Into the hideous shed.

He does not stare upon the air
 Through a little roof of glass;
He does not pray with lips of clay
 For his agony to pass;
Nor feel upon his shuddering cheek
 The kiss of Caiaphas.

II

Six weeks our guardsman walked the yard,
  In a suit of shabby grey:
His cricket cap was on his head,
  And his step seemed light and gay,
But I never saw a man who looked
  So wistfully at the day.

I never saw a man who looked
  With such a wistful eye
Upon that little tent of blue
  Which prisoners call the sky,
And at every wandering cloud that trailed
  Its ravelled fleeces by.

He did not wring his hands, as do
  Those witless men who dare
To try to rear the changeling Hope
  In the cave of black Despair:
He only looked upon the sun,
  And drank the morning air.

He did not wring his hands nor weep,
  Nor did he peek or pine,
But he drank the air as though it held
  Some healthful anodyne;
With open mouth he drank the sun
  As though it had been wine!

And I and all the souls in pain,
  Who tramped the other ring,
Forgot if we ourselves had done
  A great or little thing,
And watched with gaze of dull amaze
  The man who had to swing.

And strange it was to see him pass
  With a step so light and gay,
And strange it was to see him look
  So wistfully at the day,
And strange it was to think that he
  Had such a debt to pay.

For oak and elm have pleasant leaves
  That in the spring-time shoot:
But grim to see is the gallows-tree,
  With its adder-bitten root,
And, green or dry, a man must die
  Before it bears its fruit!

The loftiest place is that seat of grace
  For which all worldlings try:
But who would stand in hempen band
  Upon a scaffold high,
And through a murderer's collar take
  His last look at the sky?

It is sweet to dance to violins
  When Love and Life are fair:
To dance to flutes, to dance to lutes
  Is delicate and rare:
But it is not sweet with nimble feet
  To dance upon the air!

So with curious eyes and sick surmise
  We watched him day by day,
And wondered if each one of us
  Would end the self-same way,
For none can tell to what red Hell
  His sightless soul may stray.

At last the dead man walked no more
  Amongst the Trial Men,
And I knew that he was standing up
  In the black dock's dreadful pen,
And that never would I see his face
  In God's sweet world again.

Like two doomed ships that pass in storm
  We had crossed each other's way:
But we made no sign, we said no word,
  We had no word to say;
For we did not meet in the holy night,
  But in the shameful day.

A prison wall was round us both,
  Two outcast men we were:
The world had thrust us from its heart,
  And God from out His care:
And the iron gin that waits for Sin
  Had caught us in its snare.

III

In Debtors' Yard the stones are hard,
  And the dripping wall is high,
So it was there he took the air
  Beneath the leaden sky,
And by each side a Warder walked,
  For fear the man might die.

Or else he sat with those who watched
  His anguish night and day;
Who watched him when he rose to weep,
  And when he crouched to pray;
Who watched him lest himself should rob
  Their scaffold of its prey.

The Governor was strong upon
  The Regulations Act:
The Doctor said that Death was but
  A scientific fact:
And twice a day the Chaplain called
  And left a little tract.

And twice a day he smoked his pipe,
  And drank his quart of beer:
His soul was resolute, and held
  No hiding-place for fear;
He often said that he was glad
  The hangman's hands were near.

But why he said so strange a thing
  No Warder dared to ask:
For he to whom a watcher's doom
  Is given as his task,
Must set a lock upon his lips,
  And make his face a mask.

Or else he might be moved, and try
  To comfort or console:
And what should Human Pity do
  Pent up in Murderers' Hole?
What word of grace in such a place
  Could help a brother's soul?

With slouch and swing around the ring
  We trod the Fool's Parade!
We did not care: we knew we were
  The Devil's Own Brigade:
And shaven head and feet of lead
  Make a merry masquerade.

We tore the tarry rope to shreds
  With blunt and bleeding nails;
We rubbed the doors, and scrubbed the floors,
  And cleaned the shining rails:
And, rank by rank, we soaped the plank,
  And clattered with the pails.

We sewed the sacks, we broke the stones,
  We turned the dusty drill:
We banged the tins, and bawled the hymns,
  And sweated on the mill:
But in the heart of every man
  Terror was lying still.

So still it lay that every day
  Crawled like a weed-clogged wave:
And we forgot the bitter lot
  That waits for fool and knave,
Till once, as we tramped in from work,
  We passed an open grave.

With yawning mouth the yellow hole
  Gaped for a living thing;
The very mud cried out for blood
  To the thirsty asphalte ring:
And we knew that ere one dawn grew fair
  Some prisoner had to swing.

Right in we went, with soul intent
  On Death and Dread and Doom:
The hangman, with his little bag,
  Went shuffling through the gloom
And each man trembled as he crept
  Into his numbered tomb.

That night the empty corridors
  Were full of forms of Fear,
And up and down the iron town
  Stole feet we could not hear,
And through the bars that hide the stars
  White faces seemed to peer.

He lay as one who lies and dreams
  In a pleasant meadow-land,
The watcher watched him as he slept,
  And could not understand
How one could sleep so sweet a sleep
  With a hangman close at hand?

But there is no sleep when men must weep
  Who never yet have wept:
So we—the fool, the fraud, the knave—
  That endless vigil kept,
And through each brain on hands of pain
  Another's terror crept.

Alas! it is a fearful thing
  To feel another's guilt!
For, right within, the sword of Sin
  Pierced to its poisoned hilt,
And as molten lead were the tears we shed
  For the blood we had not spilt.

The Warders with their shoes of felt
  Crept by each padlocked door,
And peeped and saw, with eyes of awe,
  Grey figures on the floor,
And wondered why men knelt to pray
  Who never prayed before.

All through the night we knelt and prayed,
  Mad mourners of a corse!
The troubled plumes of midnight were
  The plumes upon a hearse:
And bitter wine upon a sponge
  Was the saviour of Remorse.

The grey cock crew, the red cock crew,
  But never came the day:
And crooked shape of Terror crouched,
  In the corners where we lay:
And each evil sprite that walks by night
  Before us seemed to play.

They glided past, they glided fast,
  Like travellers through a mist:
They mocked the moon in a rigadoon
  Of delicate turn and twist,
And with formal pace and loathsome grace
  The phantoms kept their tryst.

With mop and mow, we saw them go,
  Slim shadows hand in hand:
About, about, in ghostly rout
  They trod a saraband:
And the damned grotesques made arabesques,
  Like the wind upon the sand!

With the pirouettes of marionettes,
  They tripped on pointed tread:
But with flutes of Fear they filled the ear,
  As their grisly masque they led,
And loud they sang, and long they sang,
  For they sang to wake the dead.

'Oho!' they cried, 'The world is wide,
  But fettered limbs go lame!
And once, or twice, to throw the dice
  Is a gentlemanly game,
But he does not win who plays with Sin
  In the secret House of Shame.'

No things of air these antics were
  That frolicked with such glee:
To men whose lives were held in gyves,
  And whose feet might not go free,
Ah! wounds of Christ! they were living things,
  Most terrible to see.

Around, around, they waltzed and wound;
  Some wheeled in smirking pairs:
With the mincing step of demirep
  Some sidled up the stairs:
And with subtle sneer, and fawning leer,
  Each helped us at our prayers.

The morning wind began to moan,
  But still the night went on:
Through its giant loom the web of gloom
  Crept till each thread was spun:
And, as we prayed, we grew afraid
  Of the Justice of the Sun.

The moaning wind went wandering round
  The weeping prison-wall:
Till like a wheel of turning-steel
  We felt the minutes crawl:
O moaning wind! what had we done
  To have such a seneschal?

At last I saw the shadowed bars
  Like a lattice wrought in lead,
Move right across the whitewashed wall
  That faced my three-plank bed,
And I knew that somewhere in the world
  God's dreadful dawn was red.

At six o'clock we cleaned our cells,
  At seven all was still,
But the sough and swing of a mighty wing
  The prison seemed to fill,
For the Lord of Death with icy breath
  Had entered in to kill.

He did not pass in purple pomp,
  Nor ride a moon-white steed.
Three yards of cord and a sliding board
  Are all the gallows need:
So with rope of shame the Herald came
  To do the secret deed.

We were as men who through a fen
  Of filthy darkness grope:
We did not dare to breathe a prayer,
  Or give our anguish scope:
Something was dead in each of us,
  And what was dead was Hope.

For Man's grim Justice goes its way,
  And will not swerve aside:
It slays the weak, it slays the strong,
  It has a deadly stride:
With iron heel it slays the strong,
  The monstrous parricide!

We waited for the stroke of eight:
  Each tongue was thick with thirst:
For the stroke of eight is the stroke of Fate
  That makes a man accursed,
And Fate will use a running noose
  For the best man and the worst.

We had no other thing to do,
  Save to wait for the sign to come:
So, like things of stone in a valley lone,
  Quiet we sat and dumb:
But each man's heart beat thick and quick
  Like a madman on a drum!

With sudden shock the prison-clock
  Smote on the shivering air,
And from all the gaol rose up a wail
  Of impotent despair,
Like the sound that frightened marshes hear
  From a leper in his lair.

And as one sees most dreadful things
  In the crystal of a dream,
We saw the greasy hempen rope
  Hooked to the blackened beam,
And heard the prayer the hangman's snare
  Strangled into a scream.

And all the woe that moved him so
  That he gave that bitter cry,
And the wild regrets, and the bloody sweats,
  None knew so well as I:
For he who lives more lives than one
  More deaths than one must die.

IV

There is no chapel on the day
  On which they hang a man:
The Chaplain's heart is far too sick,
  Or his face is far too wan,
Or there is that written in his eyes
  Which none should look upon.

So they kept us close till nigh on noon,
  And then they rang the bell,
And the Warders with their jingling keys
  Opened each listening cell,
And down the iron stair we tramped,
  Each from his separate Hell.

Out into God's sweet air we went,
  But not in wonted way,
For this man's face was white with fear,
  And that man's face was grey,
And I never saw sad men who looked
  So wistfully at the day.

I never saw sad men who looked
  With such a wistful eye
Upon that little tent of blue
  We prisoners called the sky,
And at every careless cloud that passed
  In happy freedom by.

But there were those amongst us all
  Who walked with downcast head,
And knew that, had each got his due,
  They should have died instead:
He had but killed a thing that lived
  Whilst they had killed the dead.

For he who sins a second time
  Wakes a dead soul to pain,
And draws it from its spotted shroud,
  And makes it bleed again,
And makes it bleed great gouts of blood
  And makes it bleed in vain!

Like ape or clown, in monstrous garb
  With crooked arrows starred,
Silently we went round and round
  The slippery asphalte yard;
Silently we went round and round,
  And no man spoke a word.

Silently we went round and round,
  And through each hollow mind
The memory of dreadful things
  Rushed like a dreadful wind,
And Horror stalked before each man,
  And terror crept behind.

The Warders strutted up and down,
  And watched their herd of brutes,
Their uniforms were spick and span,
  And they wore their Sunday suits,
But we knew the work they had been at
  By the quicklime on their boots.

For where a grave had opened wide,
  There was no grave at all:
Only a stretch of mud and sand
  By the hideous prison-wall,
And a little heap of burning lime,
  That the man should have his pall.

For he has a pall, this wretched man,
  Such as few men can claim:
Deep down below a prison-yard,
  Naked for greater shame,
He lies, with fetters on each foot,
  Wrapt in a sheet of flame!

And all the while the burning lime
  Eats flesh and bone away,
It eats the brittle bone by night,
  And the soft flesh by the day,
It eats the flesh and bones by turns,
  But it eats the heart alway.

For three long years they will not sow
  Or root or seedling there:
For three long years the unblessed spot
  Will sterile be and bare,
And look upon the wondering sky
  With unreproachful stare.

They think a murderer's heart would taint
  Each simple seed they sow.
It is not true! God's kindly earth
  Is kindlier than men know,
And the red rose would but blow more red,
  The white rose whiter blow.

Out of his mouth a red, red rose!
  Out of his heart a white!
For who can say by what strange way,
  Christ brings his will to light,
Since the barren staff the pilgrim bore
  Bloomed in the great Pope's sight?

But neither milk-white rose nor red
  May bloom in prison air;
The shard, the pebble, and the flint,
  Are what they give us there:
For flowers have been known to heal
  A common man's despair.

So never will wine-red rose nor white,
  Petal by petal, fall
On that stretch of mud and sand that lies
  By the hideous prison-wall,
To tell the men who tramp the yard
  That God's Son died for all.

Yet though the hideous prison-wall
  Still hems him round and round,
And a spirit may not walk by night
  That is with fetters bound,
And a spirit may not weep that lies
  In such unholy ground,

He is at peace—this wretched man—
  At peace, or will be soon:
There is no thing to make him mad,
  Nor does Terror walk at noon,
For the lampless Earth in which he lies
  Has neither Sun nor Moon.

They hanged him as a beast is hanged:
  They did not even toll
A requiem that might have brought
  Rest to his startled soul,
But hurriedly they took him out,
  And hid him in a hole.

They stripped him of his canvas clothes,
  And gave him to the flies;
They mocked the swollen purple throat
  And the stark and staring eyes:
And with laughter loud they heaped the shroud
  In which their convict lies.

The Chaplain would not kneel to pray
  By his dishonored grave:
Nor mark it with that blessed Cross
  That Christ for sinners gave,
Because the man was one of those
  Whom Christ came down to save.

Yet all is well; he has but passed
  To Life's appointed bourne:
And alien tears will fill for him
  Pity's long-broken urn,
For his mourners will be outcast men,
  And outcasts always mourn.

V

I know not whether Laws be right,
　Or whether Laws be wrong;
All that we know who lie in gaol
　Is that the wall is strong;
And that each day is like a year,
　A year whose days are long.

But this I know, that every Law
　That men have made for Man,
Since first Man took his brother's life,
　And the sad world began,
But straws the wheat and saves the chaff
　With a most evil fan.

This too I know—and wise it were
　If each could know the same—
That every prison that men build
　Is built with bricks of shame,
And bound with bars lest Christ should see
　How men their brothers maim.

With bars they blur the gracious moon,
　And blind the goodly sun:
And they do well to hide their Hell,
　For in it things are done
That Son of God nor son of Man
　Ever should look upon!

The vilest deeds like poison weeds
　Bloom well in prison-air:
It is only what is good in Man
　That wastes and withers there:
Pale Anguish keeps the heavy gate,
　And the Warder is Despair

For they starve the little frightened child
  Till it weeps both night and day:
And they scourge the weak, and flog the fool,
  And gibe the old and grey,
And some grow mad, and all grow bad,
  And none a word may say.

Each narrow cell in which we dwell
  Is a foul and dark latrine,
And the fetid breath of living Death
  Chokes up each grated screen,
And all, but Lust, is turned to dust
  In Humanity's machine.

The brackish water that we drink
  Creeps with a loathsome slime,
And the bitter bread they weigh in scales
  Is full of chalk and lime,
And Sleep will not lie down, but walks
  Wild-eyed and cries to Time.

But though lean Hunger and green Thirst
  Like asp with adder fight,
We have little care of prison fare,
  For what chills and kills outright
Is that every stone one lifts by day
  Becomes one's heart by night.

With midnight always in one's heart,
  And twilight in one's cell,
We turn the crank, or tear the rope,
  Each in his separate Hell,
And the silence is more awful far
  Than the sound of a brazen bell.

And never a human voice comes near
  To speak a gentle word:
And the eye that watches through the door
  Is pitiless and hard:
And by all forgot, we rot and rot,
  With soul and body marred.

And thus we rust Life's iron chain
  Degraded and alone:
And some men curse, and some men weep,
  And some men make no moan:
But God's eternal Laws are kind
  And break the heart of stone.

And every human heart that breaks,
  In prison-cell or yard,
Is as that broken box that gave
  Its treasure to the Lord,
And filled the unclean leper's house
  With the scent of costliest nard.

Ah! happy day they whose hearts can break
  And peace of pardon win!
How else may man make straight his plan
  And cleanse his soul from Sin?
How else but through a broken heart
  May Lord Christ enter in?

And he of the swollen purple throat.
  And the stark and staring eyes,
Waits for the holy hands that took
  The Thief to Paradise;
And a broken and a contrite heart
  The Lord will not despise.

The man in red who reads the Law
  Gave him three weeks of life,
Three little weeks in which to heal
  His soul of his soul's strife,
And cleanse from every blot of blood
  The hand that held the knife.

And with tears of blood he cleansed the hand,
  The hand that held the steel:
For only blood can wipe out blood,
  And only tears can heal:
And the crimson stain that was of Cain
  Became Christ's snow-white seal.

VI

In Reading gaol by Reading town
  There is a pit of shame,
And in it lies a wretched man
  Eaten by teeth of flame,
In burning winding-sheet he lies,
  And his grave has got no name.

And there, till Christ call forth the dead,
  In silence let him lie:
No need to waste the foolish tear,
  Or heave the windy sigh:
The man had killed the thing he loved,
  And so he had to die.

And all men kill the thing they love,
  By all let this be heard,
Some do it with a bitter look,
  Some with a flattering word,
The coward does it with a kiss,
  The brave man with a sword!

Gareth Armstrong has combined the roles of actor, director, writer and teacher throughout a career that has taken him to over fifty countries. He has been a member of the RSC, worked at Shakespeare's Globe and in the West End. He has directed a wide repertoire of work all over the UK as well as in Europe and America. He wrote his own one-man show, *Shylock*, which toured internationally for ten years. Since then he has worked with writers and actors to create solo theatre pieces for other performers. He records audiobooks, video games and has played three different running characters in *The Archers*. His published work includes *A Case for Shylock – Around the World with Shakespeare's Jew* and an instructional book for actors, *So You Want To Do A Solo Show*, both published by Nick Hern Books. *www.garetharmstrong.com*

Gerard Logan trained at the Royal Academy of Dramatic Art, where he won the Bancroft Gold Medal. As well as leading roles in TV, film and radio, he has played classical and contemporary theatre roles with the Royal Shakespeare Company (where he received an Olivier Award nomination), the National Theatre, in the West End and with numerous leading provincial theatres. He won *The Stage*'s 'Best Solo Performer' Award at the 2011 Edinburgh Festival for his performance in Shakespeare's great narrative poem *The Rape of Lucrece* which, alongside *Wilde Without the Boy* and *The Ballad of Reading Gaol,* he is currently touring internationally. He won the 'Best Actor' award at the Buxton Fringe Theatre Festival in 2104 for his performance in *Wilde Without the Boy*. *www.gerardlogan.com*

Simon Slater has composed original music for over 200 theatre, film, television and radio productions – a career which he has pursued in parallel with the life of a busy actor. Recently he has provided music for the award-winning *Constellations* (Duke of York's, London, and Royal Court, New York) for which he was nominated for an Olivier award, *Carmen Disruption* by Simon Stephens (Almeida) and *The Broken Heart* (Globe). Other musical credits include *Tis Pity She's a Whore* (Globe), *Great Expectations* (Vaudeville Theatre), *Arabian Nights* (Sherman, Cardiff), *Ghosts* (New Vic), *Land of Our Fathers* and *Handful of Stars* (Trafalgar Studios and Theatre 503) - nominated for 2 Off West awards. *Cannibals* (Royal Exchange Manchester), *Two Men of Florence* by Richard N Goodwin (Huntington Theatre, Boston), *Romeo and Juliet* (Royal Shakespeare Company), *Henry V* and *Julius Caesar* (Royal Shakespeare Company), *Macbeth* (Albery, West End), *Rose Rage* (Chicago Shakespeare Theatre and Duke Theatre, New York). *www.slatermusic.com*

Designed by Stephen Davies
in Minion and Cronos